RESURRECTION

RESURRECTION

poems by
NICOLE COOLEY

LOUISIANA STATE UNIVERSITY PRESS
Baton Rouge and London 1996

Designer: Glynnis Weston
Typeface: Trajan and Granjon
Typesetter: Impressions Book and Journal Services, Inc.
Printer and binder: Thomson-Shore, Inc.

Grateful acknowledgment is made to the editors of the following publications, in which the poems listed first appeared, sometimes in slightly different versions: *Antioch Review*, "Rio de Janeiro"; *Field*, "Diane Arbus, New York"; *Indiana Review*, "The New World"; *The Nation*, "The Family History," "Maison Blanche," "Romance," "Self-Portrait: Frida Kahlo"; *New England Review and Breadloaf Quarterly*, "The Red Shoes"; *Poetry*, "Undine"; *Poetry Northwest*, "For My Sister"; *Quarterly West*, "Patty Hearst: A Love Poem"; *Seattle Review*, "No Private History"; *Southern Poetry Review*, "Letter from the Louisiana Women's Prison" (as "Letter from the Arizona Women's Prison"); *Virginia Quarterly Review*, "Alice Changing Size in the Hall of Doors," "Noli Me Tangere"; and *Willow Springs*, "Alice in Paradise," "Good Friday, Alice Liddell." "Confession" originally appeared in *Ploughshares*, XXI, No. 1.

The author would like to thank the Corporation of Yaddo and the Ragdale Foundation for the generous support that enabled the writing of these poems. For their sustaining encouragement of her work, the author also wants to thank Pamela Barnett, Alissa Cooley, Jacqueline Cooley, Peter Cooley, Amelie Hastie, Mary Leader, Anne Marks, Gretchen Mattox, Janet McAdams, Tom Whalen, and, most especially, Alexander Hinton.

Library of Congress Cataloging-in-Publication Data

Cooley, Nicole.
   Resurrection : poems / by Nicole Cooley.
      p.   cm.
   "Winner of the Walt Whitman Award for 1995."
   ISBN 0-8071-2058-8 (c : alk. paper). — ISBN 0-8071-2059-6 (p :
alk. paper)
   I. Title.
PS3553.05647R47   1996
811'.54—dc20   96-2242
                                           CIP

The paper in this book meets the guidelines for permanence and durability of the Committee on Production Guidelines for Book Longevity of the Council on Library Resources. ∞

WINNER OF THE WALT WHITMAN AWARD FOR 1995

Sponsored by The Academy of American Poets, the Walt Whitman Award is given annually to the winner of an open competition among American poets who have not yet published a first book of poems.

Judge for 1995: Cynthia Macdonald

FOR MY MOTHER AND FATHER

Claire, if I speak of the smell of garrets, it is for memory's sake. And of the twin beds where two sisters fall asleep, dreaming of one another.
                              —Jean Genet, *The Maids*

in that most dangerous place, the family home
we were the chosen people

In the beginning we grasp whatever we can.
                              —Adrienne Rich, "Sources"

CONTENTS

Hunger   1

I   NOLI ME TANGERE

II   THE NEW WORLD

III   THE LAST CHILD OF THE TWENTIETH CENTURY

RESURRECTION

HUNGER

In the unnamed village the priest breaks the Body
of Christ above the child who will become my great-grandmother.
The baptism is complete with the Bread of Heaven, the bread
other women shape into loaves to bring luck, good fortune
to be passed through her body into the bloodline to her unborn
children like water leaking from the fields through
the dirt floor of the house. By now, at the end of the century,
it's clear you're not coming back for us. You're not returning
to save us, and my inheritance is the wish for nothing
but emptiness. I cast my lot with the women in my family.
I follow them. I choose the rituals of grief.
Again and again the boat crosses the ocean from Europe
to America, then back, and I am running. I circle
the block where you once lived, the house
I can't enter, where my aunt and my mother lie
side by side in the dark in your bed. I run until
my muscles burn. Your granddaughters will sleep together
in this house for the rest of their lives.
The day you leave Budapest, meat hangs in the market,
a lamb skinned and strung up by its front legs, body
slit open. Steam rises from its belly, from the space
between its back legs. Is this the moment when it began?
When you vowed to fast, to turn your body pure, immaculate
like Mary, to prepare yourself for the kind of love
that accompanies refusal and holds sisters together?
I circle the block again and again till my breath catches
in my throat. If you believe the dead send messages,
here is your punishment—all of us hoping to become
children, hoping for safety. We will do anything
to prevent the panic that stutters in the chest,
anything to keep ourselves hollow and flat.
Inside your house my mother spoons milk
into her sister's mouth. They sit silently at your table.
I circle the block, holding my breath. My mother drinks
glass after glass of vinegar on ice to fill her stomach
with the pain that's familiar, the pain that we love.
When we finally find you in the afterlife, will we be pure
enough for you? At night in my own house I lay
the table, crystal plates and saucers, three forks for each
guest, a spoon set above every place. There is room for all

of the women at the table. I serve the objects that promise luck:
pigeon feathers and coffee beans for love, ten-cent babies to signal
fertility. I pile pennies on each plate for prosperity.
Here is a stone from the bottom of the sea you crossed.
Lay it flat on your tongue. Pass it from one to the other
in your mouths. At the end of the century I will step out
of my body like a dress, leave it on the floor.
Rose, I want to speak with your voice in the language
none of us understands. I want your kiss, your tongue
in my mouth. This is not love but how we inherit
each other. I sit alone at the table, notebook open on my lap.
Listen. I am the one who will tell about it.

I   NOLI ME TANGERE

ROMANCE

On the train to New Orleans my sister and I
light the Virgen de Guadalupe candles
and the line of unlucky women steps out from the flame.

They file past at the window where we sit,
where we have given up being safe from them,
our four aunts with their loose dresses for mourning,

their fasting, their silent refusals. These women loved
their grief like the bread they would not let themselves eat,
like the children they would not allow into their bodies.

We know their unspoken lesson—take nothing
into the body. We know they will wait for us,
a line of dolls cut from the same sheet of butcher paper,

the sisters of this family linked by their hands and alone.
One mile into Mississippi, the train passes a statue
of blue-robed Mary in someone else's yard, bathtubs leaning

against the wire fence. I place us there. With relief,
I lower each of us into the bath, into the crystal salts.
Oil pools on the surface of the water. Sulfur is staining our skin.

The train drags on across the tracks, away from us,
leaving us in our own story. My first aunt looks down
at the flat pan of her pelvis, strung tight between hipbones

she'll never touch. She likes her body empty and clean.
Coaxing her into the tub, we preach the virtues of this water,
its power to wash away sin. The second one taps

her cigarette ash on the grass and blows smoke at the sky
while we plead with her about drowning,
tell her not to go all the way down. Why should she listen?

We know how good the body can feel, unused, expecting
nothing. But my sister and I are trying to prove them wrong.
When I kneel beside my family, I am desperate.

My sister drags the sign of the cross in the dirt
with a stick. Why don't we quit telling the story?
Once upon a time there were four princesses and a single

safe tower. No prince. In place of a man, a basket
of primroses they ripped into pieces, four finches
fighting it out for the kingdom. In another story,

my sister and I take them all home to New Orleans.
I take them all into me, my secret collection.
I give up. They live in my body. Oh, we are beautiful.

In the real story, we are all starving together. Sisters,
the wafer floats on my tongue like bad luck, like our name.

SELF-PORTRAIT: FRIDA KAHLO

I hope for a happy exit and I hope never to come back.
—last entry in the diary of Frida Kahlo, 1954

I

The women sprinkle holy water on the sidewalk
as they pass the house where Diego painted
the courtyard walls, volcanic stone from San Angel.

Inside Casa Azul the blue parrot chases hens
and she begins the long ceremony of dressing:
rings studding the fingers of both hands, earrings

of heavy gold filigree hung to her shoulders,
bougainvillaea to wind and unwind in her hair.
Last, the skirt arranged to hide the orthopedic shoe.

The women know the stories of the hospitals
and the x-rays that shot light through her bones,
illuminating nothing. They speak of the children she refused

to let live in her body, how she chose instead the metal rod
fused in her spine. They have never seen her paintings
but they say the rosary in her name while she lies in the canopy

bed under her photographs of Marx, Engels, Chairman Mao.
If you enter that house, the women know, she'll show you
her collection of dolls and curios that line the walls,

the *bolero* she bought the afternoon of the accident.
If you enter that house, you'll see the fetus in a jar
of formaldehyde she will present as her own child.

They know she does not dwell in the House of the Lord.
Her house must belong to the penitent Mother, the stone
virgin in Juarez who cries real tears, reported on the radio.

II

He is a man who can open water with his hands,
the second accident of my life. For the first I wear

7

the corset painted with vines and flowers. For Diego
I make an effigy of papier-mâché, Frida

in a fringed *rebozo*, a doll to be burned as an offering
during Lent. In the hospital we fold paper into parts

for the Exquisite Corpse game. Together we draw
a body. I sketch a thorn necklace circling a pair

of breasts, a monkey crouching on a woman's naked
back. Each night he watches me drink from the cup

of white liquid that will light my body for the surgeons,
my spine a flash, a broken column of lightning.

I wish that lightning could erase my body.
To disappear, I paint my portrait again and again.

III

When I enter the Casa Azul Museum, I find her diary
left open on the kitchen table. An unfinished portrait
of Trotsky waits at the easel. Exhibited on the bed,
the plaster corset testifies to her pain. I want to know

that pain. I want to save her as Diego could not.
The women say he gathered her ashes in a scarf.
He gathered her up at the end of her life. I want
to hold her as he once did, as if that embrace

could knit the spine together. I want to slip
into her clothes, pulling the embroidered skirt over my knees
while her cigarette turns to ash between my fingers.
The blue parrot perches on my shoulder. The spider

monkey hides at my feet. To save her, I leave
the museum. I carry her dolls from the house
to the Avenida Juarez, holding the wire ribs, the faces
built of strips of plaster, wrapped in her necklaces,

her petticoats, her shawls. I want to hold her.
In honor of her, I set our bodies burning, burning.
Our grief lights up the avenue.

NO PRIVATE HISTORY

Like finding other people's postcards
in your own desk drawer, your sisters' faces
are appearing in your dreams.
Janet married the hardware man
but still her hands could hold you,
touch your hair as gently as they'd slice
her butter cake or her treasured bread,
as they'd arrange your mother's cut-glass
canisters along the kitchen wall.
She's not the type to serve her guests
iced tea. She never writes you
anymore. Then there's Linda, teaching
kindergarten in North Miami Beach, the one
who knew the name for everything.
On car rides as a child you cried
because she won each game you played—
she knew the name of the Fred Astaire
Dance Studio, the Spanish word for grapefruit,
the color to describe the Illinois morning sky.
She collected words like jacks or rubber balls.

Outside at the edge of your lawn,
at the edge of each morning, you touch
the mailbox's metal tongue. You wait.

Grace was nothing like her name.
You know you'll never hear from her,
although she told you all her secrets
at sixteen, then ran away without a note.
She sent your mother two postcards from motels
in Kansas towns. Once she said she planned
to practice magic with a troupe of traveling mimes.

Why are they still here, so stuck
in your brain, where they loom larger
even than those family portraits
your mother kept preserved in a forbidden room?
They want to lean out of their frames,

they want to speak to you. Or do they dream
without trying to think back? Who took
your picture from their lives, left
the repeating absence of an empty frame?

ALICE CHANGING SIZE
IN THE HALL OF DOORS

Even now, my father's voice travels far
  In the silence and my mother is driving

Away from us, growing smaller, smaller.
  My mother is about to disappear.

I could take you there, to where the story
  Opens, to the house where each night

I waited for my father to begin, locked the door,
  Pushed my rocking chair under the knob, keeping us

Safe, lit two blue candles, spread my mother's good white cloth
  Over the table like the sheet stretched flat

Across the bed she never slept in. My father sleeps
  All day, in my bed, a bed he is too big for.

He curls his body, tries to make himself smaller
  In his sleep. I listen for his breathing,

Touch his shoulder, his damp skin, to wake him,
  Say *it's time*, lead him to the table where,

Between us, on the cloth, I fill the water glass
  With whiskey. I know how much to pour, how to hide

The bottle and the book together beneath my mother's bed.
  There is no place for you at the table.

Stand back. Stay here. I will let you listen.
  I will show you how we leave this house, my father and I

Alone together, as he begins to read. The candles sputter,
  Flicker, burn. We are so safe

Without my mother. My father drinks slowly,
  His voice filling the room, rising along the walls.

There is this stillness, heat, a haze that shimmers
            In the grass. In the boat, Alice sits shaded

By the haycocks, by the faint wind that blows like breath
            Over the lake. Dressed in white the Reverend Dodgson rows.

He takes off his straw hat, begins. He invents
            The story as he goes along.

My father and I fall, fall slowly
            In the dark. Together we turn, spin to the center

Of the earth. Cupboards line the tunnel walls.
            There are books, glass bottles, watercolor maps.

My father points down a long, low hall, lit
            By a row of lamps. He shows me the three-legged table

Made of solid glass, the tiny golden key.
            On the lake the boat drifts as the story ends.

Alice turns toward the shore, toward home.
            The oars cut the surface of the dark water.

I hold my father's hand. We stand so still.
            This is the beginning of another story.

My father cannot enter the hall of doors.
            He cannot fold his body up to fit inside.

Behind one of those doors, there are blue flowers, crystal
            Fountains, there is a garden, open sky.

Tell me, did he want me to leave him,
            To grow smaller, larger, to grow up, to disappear?

LETTER FROM THE
LOUISIANA WOMEN'S PRISON

It was done as quick and clean
as slipping a stone into water.
Don't you know I would take him
to the river? Past the levee,
to the uneven gravel edge.
I wanted the water turning
its back to us like you would,
the wind leading our voices
backward in a separate direction.

You have to imagine this—
I pulled him down with me
to kneel by the rocks, touched his head
to the ground. River mud left a stain
above his eyes. I told him to walk into the water.
I told him I would follow,
then I pushed him down.
His hair like wet leaves
between my fingers. I wanted to say,
I wouldn't hold you if I could,
but I repeated his name three times
like a prayer. Your boy—
never any part of me.
Was I pretending he was you?

When I came to show you
what I had done, I wanted to make
a gift to you, a piece of hair
or the cut-off hands, fingers I pulled
out like tiny plants.

You've got to come and get me now.
Nothing will rise between us.
Your hands can reach for me,
lock your body over mine.
Don't talk,
your mouth to my throat.
If you leave me now you know
you'll leave your blood behind.

PATTY HEARST: A LOVE POEM

I

The other women wear my clothes,
pose in the doorway.
The blonde one tightens
the belt of your robe, the robe they took me in.
Don't look at me. Keep your head down.

Sister, the rag is knotted in my mouth and I can't call to you.
When I speak into the tape recorder,
I say the words that might spell freedom—
Mom, Dad, I'm okay—my face pushed to the floor.
Your name does not exist in my new language.

In the new story, the king of the castle wants to keep
the people starving, to keep the people out.
Our Father, who art in heaven, I repeat. Our father
is the enemy. The women are watching.
I cover my breasts with my hands.

II

Behind the blindfold the world is stopped, a darkened movie screen.
It's only a closet. I curl my knees to my chest. It's only the trunk of a car.

It's a trash can with two holes the size of dimes
cut out for me to breathe. I asked my body for safety and safety

meant nothing. I ask my body to remember you and I find
the family sitting at the long table, Father at one end alone,

asking the polite questions, the easy ones to answer.
But that's not the moment I want back. I want the two of us

sleeping in a single bed, your arms wrapped around my shoulders.
Your hands are pale fish, cool against my skin.

You breathe evenly, sleeping the sleep of safe children.

III

If grief is a contest, Sister, I am winning.
In the lit-up house on the hill, you know that I am dead.
But you don't know what *surrender* means.

In the safehouse there are no refusals.
You don't know the forgiving of the body
as each man enters me again and again.

When I swallow the sleeping draught,
I see the chalice, Mother at the altar,
cupping the communion wafer in her hands.
Does she know she is the enemy?
The priest's blessing sticks in my throat like a gag.

I am the dutiful one, the princess taking directions.
I am crossing over without you.
Don't look at me.

IV

I imagine you here, wearing the gas mask,
preparing for the storming of the safehouse.

In this story, Father's army will blow the house down.
You will not be afraid. You divide the combat rations carefully,
practice one hundred push-ups to make your body strong.

You hold my face in your hands to line the insides of my eyes.

Show me how to become someone else—

V

There is nothing anyone can do
to prepare for the unknown.
To prepare for the war, I memorize the codes in the rule book,
repeat my new name.

In the house on the hill, Mother makes the sign of the cross.
No one can comfort you.
Across the city, I swallow the unfamiliar like a cure.
I have learned the lesson of adulthood before you.
I was never a child.

SNOW WHITE

The casket lengthens with her body
in the story told by the two sisters,
storytellers of the unnamed village
where the Brothers Grimm stop for the night.

Listen, the first says, she was warned
not to open the door to anyone and three times
she invited the mad woman in, let

the Queen lace the corset to crush the breath
from her body, placed the poison comb
in her own black hair, swallowed
a piece from the magic side of the apple.

At the table in the sisters' house the men
translate each word into their own language.
The sisters' story fills page after page.

In this story, the women are condemned
to daylight, the Queen dancing the fire
dance in iron shoes, the Queen burning.
The girl's body is locked in the Prince's embrace.

Years later, in another country, my mother's sisters
accept the apple like a communion wafer:
the Body of Christ, the Bread of Heaven.

At the altar they wait, hands open, hoping
to sleep for the rest of the century while they grow
old in their deaths, apart from everyone,
and beg the Queen to return with the other

punishments, greater terrors, a promise—
this time, nothing will save you.
If they drink from the Cup of Salvation,

they can refuse the Prince and his offer
of refuge, his kingdom. In the forest
I wash my aunts' faces with wine and water.
I lay their bodies on the crystal slab.

Their eyes stay open. Nothing can carry them
into the sleep they want. Over and over I prepare
the potion to take the sisters into the other world.

They can't get enough of oblivion.

RIO DE JANEIRO

You will never understand the avenues,
you tell me, looking past my chair.
Below your balcony, the palms
lean like women in the wind,
and I hear a merchant's horses in the street.
A man dragging a straw cart
stacked with cloth and coffee beans
looks up to our window, toward the light.
You pull a rope to close the curtains,
turn on the radio inside.

This isn't your country,
you say, then remark that you have always
liked Brazilian songs. I've seen
the women who sing them, those
dancers in dark bars who throw
their long blue scarves to you,
shake strings of wooden beads,
and beckon you away.
I'll take you to the carnival,
you say, then I imagine women
in woven clothes, you winding
holiday flowers into their hair.
You asked me once to imitate their dance.

Come away from the window.
The light is fading
and will not last much longer,
the sailors at the port
will be pulling in their boats,
those men who wave their caps
and call to me through cupped hands
from the water when I am alone.
Then you spread out a map
of this city on your bed,
point out the tiled sidewalks,
the wooden houses with the secret
doors you know.

I want to ask you
why you brought me here,

why I cannot call this home,
but you turn out the light
and reach for me, and my words fall
between us like the coins
I've watched women toss to you,
each time you pass them on the road.

ESCAPES: HARRY HOUDINI

I   MARRIAGE

Husband and wife practice in the bedroom
of his mother's house. Bess fits her body
into the trunk, head folded to her knees

as if in prayer, mouth sealed with wax
so she cannot cry out. She times her breathing—
panic increases the intake of air. Tomorrow,

at the Dime Museum on Seventh Avenue,
he will resurrect this woman for the crowd,
a miracle. She is his witness. With him

she can remain below the surface of the bath.
Underwater: the two of them go down together.
The man she loves can make her body disappear.

II   FOR MY FATHER

In your sister's dreams your mouth is gagged,
your body roped to the chair, and you do not

call out. You are her prisoner. You are hers
as she once belonged to the doctors who held her

down for each punishment: bite the wire, lock
the door, drive the panic out of the body,

close the eyes until you think of nothing
but a silver milk can that contains a child.

To her, you will always be that child. In the hospital,
all night she walks the halls and remembers how she failed

at dying. Your fault. The pills in a paper cup
promise the return of the soul to the body.

Why should her soul want to return? Why not
give up and become the fine white ash, the tip

of the cigarette burning to nothing between her fingers?
She walks and sleeps and walks on the long

hall with the other women. She cannot let go
of her body. Your fault. No—for years now you

have been ready to release her.

III   WET SHEET ESCAPE

In the Orpheum's darkness
the nurses search his body for the secrets
of his escape. His wife waits
at his side, the operating table at center stage.

The nurses wind the sheets around his ribs,
bandage his ankles, tie his neck to the table.
In an assembly line
the women fill bucket after bucket
with ice water to soak the sheets.

This is the hospital's worst punishment, reserved for the hopeless.

This trick will still the body to silence, empty the mind.

This is one of the miracles of the twentieth century.

IV   THE BATH

After I fill the tub with the crystal salts, the dried yellow roses,
after I set the votive candles in a row to circle the room,

after my dress drops from my body, I begin my ritual.
This is the crystal water casket, the glass box

I return to when panic rises in my throat,
the purification trick. We have learned that we need the trick.

I want to be the woman who drives the soul out
of the body. I want to fill the tub with blocks of ice,

drag the cigarette ash over my wrist, bind my arms to my sides.
I want to live beneath the surface of this water alone,

my body never joined with another, to learn the secrets
of escape. Let me be the witness, chronicler of the other

women's escapes. Father, help me. There are no more miracles.

I speak for all of us. We want the punishment.

UNDINE

After she rose from the dark throat
of the sea, her voice, light
as a shell, calls along the water.
The fishermen wait on the shore
when she loosens her hair over wet white shoulders.
Their wives watch at the windows.

At dusk these women scrub supper fish
and set the frying pans to burn.
In their bowls of black wine
the men find Undine, arms open,
her body shearing through the ease of the dark.

She has come to land before.
She knows the urgency
of the fishermen's hands, that breath
in her ear. She leaves
an umbrella of hair on each pillow,
a shadow pale as a fish
in a cave of water. Then she will travel
through the night into the sea,
into a deeper, retrospective blue,
her mouth seeking only her own name.

GOOD FRIDAY, ALICE LIDDELL

I

The sun sticks like an aspirin in the sky.

II

Mother, I've come back for the cure, back
to the afternoons when we lie flat on the grass
in the yard to offer our bodies to God,
to offer our bodies to you.

III

In the kitchen Mother preaches denial,
tells us the tricks—lemon slices spread on the tongue,
glasses of vinegar and ice to thin out the blood.

IV

This is the one day she looks forward to all year.
This is the one day her daughters are hers.

V

Years later I will cross through the streets of another city
looking for the man who can bring me here,
to the place she invented.
You don't need the body for love.
You need refusal.
This is the Body of Christ.
This is the Bread of Heaven.
This is the thrill along my spine when I don't take him in.

VI

To reach God, Saint Rose takes in nothing.
Hunger is beautiful.
In the garden she waits to rise closer to him.

VII

I am waiting for this simple retrieval.
As the man in the bed grips my wrists,
I turn lighter and lighter in his arms
till I rise toward the yellow disc of the sun,
transparent and free.

VIII

I don't eat for days. I can't get enough of your refusal.

IX

Lifting the sheet from my shoulders,
I open the cage of my ribs to show him our secret,
the small fire at the center of my body,
the interior, ecstatic light.

X

In the story of childhood Alice has no lover.
She knows nothing of radiance.
In the story the body shuts up like a telescope.
Alice has no mother.

XI

In the bed I will open my body to God.

XII

On the kitchen sill the votive candles flicker
in their red glasses,
you singing, *Holy, holy, holy.*
I want each touch to return me to you.
Mother, enter my body like a lit-up room,
cure me with your miraculous light.

THE SECRET GARDEN

Maybe this will be the year we stay shut
up in my room, all light excluded, and I'll read to you

by the light of a lamp shaded with my nightgown edged
in red lace. I'll feed you bread soaked in milk,
holding your shoulders like a pair of hands.

Or the week we'll spend in the sleeping compartment
of the train, crossing the country from one coast

to another and back again. Our house—the bed that folds out
from the wall, the window shade pulled down to darkness.
I want the scene at the hospital: the two of us curled

in the cot, the bed with the high white bars and the paper cup
of pills we'll swallow obediently, to lower us into the exact

same sleep each night. That sleep will be the safest place
we'll find. The safest way we'll ever leave each other.
That's not how we find each other again.

It's not desire if we've moved past desire. It's collision
drawing us back when you reach for me and open my hands

to enclose you. It's not love but the golden key
from the other stories that opens the old door. The high wall protects
the interior, pumpkin seeds scattering across the grass,

the bed of nettles and bitter radishes. This is the place
where you pull me down. You lock your body over mine

and I don't break free. Where red cabbages bloom like roses,
each seed sprouting a secret, invisible heart. Our world
behind the fence excluded from the dangerous landscapes.

Our separate lives.

NOLI ME TANGERE

I

His letters must be read backwards in the mirror,
the sheets of rice paper Alice folds carefully
in a drawer so her father will not find them.

The Reverend offers an invitation: come to my room to see
the photographs. The girls in confirmation gowns lower their eyes
and blow their kisses to the camera.

These are the girls who do not know about danger,
the girls he meets in railway stations, in church,
at the seashore where he catches them alone.

He writes letters in his fairy script to be read
in secret with a magnifying glass.
These girls are learning his own language.

Once upon a time there were three sisters
and a basket of biscuits and ginger beer and croquet on the sand
with a man who asks them to sit for a photograph.

On the surface of the lake the boat drifts, directionless,
beside the bank where other children play kiss-in-the-ring.
You are a different kind of child, the Reverend Dodgson says.

The earth will open for one of the three,
taking her down the long hall to another world.
Listen, there are three sisters. This is not the story.

II

In church I pray for the sins of the fathers
visited over and over again upon the daughters.

God took back all the bad daughters on Ash Wednesday,
led them into his body, through the path of his throat.

One by one, they obediently followed into his heart.
These girls entered God completely.

Tell us a story, Our Father. Teach us to fear.

III

In our language kept secret from the others
we spoke to each other, sitting in the stairwell

of the public library, knees touching as he turned
the pages of the book of photographs in my lap.

We studied the statues of women with broken faces.
He pushed his tongue against my teeth, trying

to enter my throat. I wanted that panic, his hands
breaking into my body as the earth opened to receive me.

IV

In the other kingdom Alice learns the daughter's first lesson.
Bright star, sad one, sitting on the wooden slats
of the rowboat beside the man who says he loves you.
Pray to be your sisters, the unlucky, unchosen children.

In bed we were drifting
through the walls of the house. We floated out over the sidewalk.
The bed ran on wheels pushed by the wind along the street,
past the shuttered houses, dark, their eyes closed to us.

This was danger, I believed, and I dreamed
of the man from childhood on the library stairs.
I had turned into a liar.
When I reached for him he had nothing to tell me.

Calling your name from the bridge, I circle the lake
with the jar of ashes. Remember the priest's fingers dragging
the ash over our skin? You see, we are the girls
with the mark in the middle of our foreheads.

In the boat we lay mouth to mouth. He breathed me in.
I could not think of coming back.
Alice, I want to warn you. Alice.
Enter that water like a knife.

II · THE NEW WORLD

THE NEW WORLD

Each night at the edge of our bed the women wait,
stand in a circle, sifting rosary beads between their fingers,

waiting for my great-grandmother to begin. You sleep but I am listening.
I know the story she'll tell, the story that started at the beginning

of this century in the other world. My aunts watch you
sleeping. *You're never safe with a man.* In our family we're safe

with a mother. My first aunt smokes, ashes falling over
her prayer shawl. She is the one who first showed me the angle

of the blade to arc over the wrist, the best edge, how to mark
the skin with a scar without dying. *Come with us.*

Once, my great-grandmother stirred barley into the soup and warned me—
no man has the body of the Savior. No man can save women

like us. Once, I twisted her ring on my finger, a gift
from the husband who left her each week. I want to say,

our house is the first place I have ever felt passion, our house
where the women finally found me to tell me: of all the daughters

I am the one true disappointment, the girl who would not speak
the language they invented, the secret word for *fear*.

They are my punishment for choosing you, for choosing love
over grief. *Don't go forward.* In Hungary, the writing women drew

on each white dress, leaves laced together in a chain over every hem.
The women worked past midnight, stitching the sheets

where my great-grandmother would lay out her body—black thread
like the farmers' earth, red for a harvest, blue signifying grief.

I never lived in that country. I never saw her preparing to join the man
her father chose to stand beside her in the fields. But I know the girl

who ripped her wedding dress into strips and walked out of the old
world alone. Did she know she would become one of the women

with the immaculate bodies, one of the fugitives, exiled
from her own country? I want to tell you that some nights when you reach

for me, I feel myself in her body—the stiff skirt embroidered
by the village women, the calfskin shoes. I am saying the rosary,

I am saying your name, a word that arcs over the trees. When I call
you will come to me. Your body locks over mine and we return together

to that unnamed village at the beginning of the century. We return
to the other country to lie in the tall grass, hidden and alone.

We tear open the salt bread. We light a candle for our marriage
in the dark fields. Now, at the back of the church, the women wait.

My second aunt shakes her head, a warning: he'll leave you.
He's already leaving you now. She makes the sign of the cross

over her breasts, her prayer for me. In honor of this day,
my first aunt draws a long slow line across her wrist, waits

for the pain that's familiar, the pain she wants me to love.
When we kneel at the altar, do you hear them? Do you hear them

pleading? I take the Body of Christ, the Bread of Heaven, into
my mouth. The women are whispering. They cannot stop me. I take

you into my mouth. I hold your shoulders in my hands. I find
the scar that traces a river in your back. I find the edges of your body,

points on a map. Tonight the bed rocks like a cradle. We will enter
the next century without them. We will enter the next century

together. I'm here with you. Take me back.

DIANE ARBUS, NEW YORK

To experience a thing as beautiful means:
to experience it necessarily wrongly.
—Friedrich Nietzsche

RUSSEKS FIFTH AVENUE, 1933

My father arranges the window like a stage.
Tea-length gowns, Dior dresses, taffeta fanned
over driftwood. Faces back-lit by Chinese lanterns,
the wax women will draw crowds. He fastens a rose

to a mannequin's hair while in the Millinery Salon
Mother models the new collection, Joan Crawford coat
with a swing collar. Hand set on her hip, she poses
for the customers. The clerks are paid to watch and smile.

At home she hides my books and pushes me
outside to the street, the world of other children.
She locks the window eleven stories above the Park,
the ledge where I stand to look down at the reservoir.

In the evening the parlor is hung with smoke, cards
laid out next to the crystal glasses for gin. Mother took away
Alice in Wonderland, and I wait out the end of the night
in my parents' marble bathtub, wait in the dark.

When I step from my dress, I step outside my body.
I imagine men watching from windows all along the Avenue.

CONEY ISLAND, 1959

On the boardwalk Jack Dracula sits stiff
and straight like a Victorian child.
Twenty-eight stars are printed on his face.
An eagle flies across his chest past
the head of Christ. Inside his body the dye
will turn to poison in the sun.
At Hubert's Museum I photograph
the flea circus and the family of midgets,
but what I love most is the failed magic,
the box of mirrors holding the girl
the magician doesn't cut in half.
Congo the Jungle Creep swings

his grass skirt and swallows cigarettes,
dances on a row of kitchen knives.
On the boardwalk my camera
is my passport as I cross the border
from one world to another again and again.
I am crossing the border. Along Jack's wrist
I LOVE MONEY is written in curving script.
I hold the Rolleiflex waist-level to meet his eyes.

CENTRAL PARK, 1971

Between the trees I watch a woman
holding a monkey in a snowsuit,
cradling its body like a child.
I am photographing people

with the objects they love.
I photograph myself with my camera.
I am studying attachment.
I print each image again and again.

On a blackboard beside my bed
I list objects to photograph: a pet
crematorium, a condemned hotel,

the ocean liner from my dream—
a world of women, gleaming and white
and stacked in layers like a wedding cake

where we drink and smoke and play
cards all night. No men are watching.
The white ship is on fire and sinking

slowly and I can photograph anything
I want. Because there is no hope
I can photograph anything.

All night I ride the train under the city,
studying the faces of the passengers.
I want to startle them from sleep.

I want to take them home with me
to lie in my bed beside me as I grow
smaller. No one is watching.

I want someone to cross over with me
as light stains the film silver and the image
turns dark, unrecognizable.

CONFESSION

The Roosevelt Mineral Baths

Do you believe the proof is not in the body?
In the name of the Father, Son, and Holy Ghost,
John walks among the olive trees by the river,

looking for the women who will let him touch
their faces with his hands. At night in the park
I unwind the scarf from my hair, preparing to enter

the water. I yield to the stone tub as if I were giving
myself up for sleep. My body floats like a lozenge
in yellow light. My body has nothing to do with the world.

I want to believe in the promises of grace. Father, I want
to reach you. In the room full of salt water, Alice cannot find
the path to the shore. She knows that to pass through

to the garden is hopeless and remembers the bathing machines
for girls by the sea and his gift to her: the straw hat spinning
over the sand. Here there are no other girls, no use looking for God

or the Reverend or another way to become small for the door.
We are the brides confessing our sins to the one
who could love us, who could lead us down with him

to the other world. By the waters of baptism we want
to be buried with Christ in his death. The punishment is not
drowning but another terror—the body transfixed

in water, held still in the bath. In the garden Easter lilies nod
on their stems, the crystal fountain gleams in the sun.
The body fails to answer. The body fails again and again.

Tonight, the water will not take us to the world
every story promises, the world of forgiveness below
the sulfur water, the lake of a girl's sorrow, the pool of tears.

THE KIDNAPPING

Jimmy Hoffa, 1975

In Detroit the sky is a deep blank white,
each siren a dark scrawl
of disaster.

Inside the trunk of the car
he is restless, hands tied.
The gag sticks
in his throat like the fist
of a woman he won't love,
ever.

No, if love is a fist in the chest
then I love you,
the first one to enter my body.
I step out of my dress
in the childhood room.
At midnight I am waiting.

Mother won't enter this room.
She walks through the house
touching the doorways
with her fingers for balance
while her daughter hopes
for the boy riding his bike over the river.

As a child I dreamed the closet—
squares of bitter chocolate and bread
slipped through the keyhole,
the wedge of light under the door
that spelled the return
of daylight, the return of the men
who don't ask any questions,
who order the prisoner to bite down on the wire.

I love your clumsiness as the screen
drops from my window into the grass
and your body covers mine
on the canopy bed.

Here is the house
of my body. Tear down the walls,
enter the secret room beneath my ribs.

Across the city a man whose body no one
will know again is growing smaller
to fit in the shallow hole
of the earth in the Michigan woods.
No one will find him.

If this is love then I'm ready
to enter the next world
with you, your body locked over mine,
my breasts crushed to your chest.

All night the police cars will drag
Telegraph Road, looking for clues. All night
I'll work to turn this boy into an angel.

Now one foot sinks into the ground.
Let's go down together.

THE STORY OF ADÈLE H.

after François Truffaut

Night after night the boat docks at the floating city.
Halifax lies silent in black water when the women

with frightened eyes enter their new country.
At the bookshop Adèle buys a ream of newsprint

for a memoir and gives her name as Léopoldine.
The name ends nothing. Her sister's spirit still comes back,

drowning again and again each night. The funeral follows,
the wedding couple buried together, the bridal gown displayed

in the famous father's home. Adèle writes in her journal,
watches at the window. The two blue candles, the champagne glass

of roses, the lieutenant's photograph, cannot bring back the body
she offered to him, gave up. *I gave myself to you, now keep me.*

The women are crossing the water all night.
Adèle hides notes in his jacket, deep in the secret

pockets of his uniform shirts. Her sister's clothes
were burned. Graced with bad luck, they could not be given away.

Adèle writes all night—*I am your wife forever*—
while inside a carriage beside the ocean Lieutenant Pinson touches

the hair of another woman, offers his lips for a kiss.
The horses' hooves click on the cobblestone street

as they circle the dock. *I gave myself to you, now keep me.*
In the Bridgetown marketplace children grip her skirts,

her arms, as she tracks his regiment through dust-filled streets.
Now the story forms itself without her, and she has given up

trying to finish a sentence in another language.
In this exile Adèle does not write.

Léopoldine will not appear here in the market among
the yellow fruits and the chimes on a string, bells knocking all night.

This is the story of love gone wrong alone.
Like the bird that perches on the pagoda at the end

of the square, its plumage still bright blue in the dust of the tropics,
speaking its forgotten French name, practicing a solitary grief.

THE CRIMINAL AND THE SAINT

after Jean Genet's The Maids

We know the rooms by heart. We know
whose turn it is to be Madame, whose image
will be thrown back by the silver mirror.

Solange brushes my hair against my back.
She spits on my shoes for polish.
She doesn't want my body touching hers.

Tonight I'm Marie Antoinette in velvet,
heels clicking across the floor, my sister
kneeling before me. I'm the mistress mad

with grief for my lover on Devil's Island.
Exile to exile, I follow him, dreaming
escape. Inside the dumbwaiter Solange curls

her body like a child, hairpins held
in her mouth for a punishment.
On Madame's dressing table the Holy

Virgin opens her arms demanding
grace and the kitchen clock is set
to announce the end of every game.

Sister, you and I belong to the world
of outcasts. We scrub the tiles.
We peel the onions. We shake the rugs.

In the garret we drift separately
in our iron beds, without dreaming.
Listen at the door. Watch me through

the keyhole's wedge of light. Drop
the pills, one by one, into her tea.
You and I are the eternal couple.

We share each other's shame.
Scrub the tiles. Shake the rugs. Do
what you can to keep from dreaming

of our life. In the scarlet dress I spin
through her room. You wait for a miracle,
dragging a candle over your arm.

You touch the poison to your lips.
The murder is always interrupted, incomplete.
Oh, girl at the keyhole, climb on the stove.

Lie down on the grate of ashes
where one flame flickers and never
goes out. Sister, this will be our altar

where I'll hold you all night and we'll speak
the secret language of the poor,
we'll finish the performance of our grief.

I'm here. I'm with you. Sleep.

THE REUNION

Phnom Penh, Cambodia

I

In your letters you say that the lights go out
during the evening meal and everyone continues eating.
Everyone continues with the task
of scraping the spoon along the bowl, tearing the flat bread.
You make small talk in a language you don't understand.
You give up on trying to read anyone's expression,
the slow smiles that never leave their faces,
revealing nothing.
After a month in this country you know the questions
not to ask—the forced marches through the countryside,
the "relocation" camps, the pile of children's bones
left three kilometers outside the city.

You write, *Every day I want to come back but I won't.*
If you were here, I'd tell you home is not a place you can return from.
When the door of childhood swings open to receive you
you could be lost on the long hall of the past.

At the university, a rifle rings out, a woman stumbles in the street.
I am not to tell your mother that you've seen these things.
I remember her anxious prayers in the days before you left
as if Saint Antony gave up on the misplaced objects
fallen down the grate or behind the fence
and began his work on the lost children.

I know better. I know in the old stories
all the children find their way out of the forest.
In order to recover they must be changed forever.

After the curfew, locked in for the night
you pin the next month on the wall and sit in the dark.
Do you remember me then,
how you rocked me through the night
in the white four-poster bed in my room,
how you slept with your leg thrown over mine?
Do you know I wanted us to stay like this,
sleeping like the brother and sister in the other stories
without parents, the children who needed no one to be safe?

II

Fifteen years ago in this city the soldiers, boys with handmade guns
trained in the countryside, set each book on fire.
The new government wanted to erase the language.

The earth opened to receive the books.
The earth opened to receive the population of the country.

In America, where reflection is not a luxury, I am dreaming about passion.
I am dreaming of our language, kept secret from everyone,
your name like a wafer along my tongue.

I am thinking of you taking my breasts in your hands
as we sit, knee to knee, in the claw-footed tub.
Our bodies move underwater together; our legs are wings.

If I had looked down below the surface of that green water,
if I had looked down past our bodies, through our skin,
I might have seen the other world

where you live now, the world of horror
I cannot let myself imagine.

III

I hold this street of straw-roofed houses in my hands
and you stare back at me, defiant, squinting into the sun.

Beside you, with a bag of stones, a child clowns for the camera.
You say children are the best guides to follow through this city.

In my favorite story I watch you depart from the top of the tower.
I climb into our bed and sleep for the rest of the century until you return.

IV

When the angel came to us in the bathtub
we should have followed her down together
through the latticed silver drain to the other world.

When the angel sat on the edge of the bed to watch us
we should have accepted her gift, let her lead us to the highest point
of the sky where the world flattens like a map.

She would have shown us the distance that we could not cross.
She would have placed her body between us, a warning.

V

Leaving the castle, the witch has given up on finding the lost children.
How can I remember enough to keep you here?
I can keep you under this city with me.
I can see our bodies growing together in the earth,
the bones like vines on a fence, turning in on each other.
In this way we will lose our loneliness.
Can you find the path shining straight to the center of the earth
where I drop my letters, my kisses, sending them to you?
On our separate sides of the map,
we are finding our way back to each other
through earth, water, the small flame, the struck-out match,
the single light at the beginning of the world.

THE RED SHOES

It's always there—the world you did not believe in.

Now, without you, I will travel back
              to childhood, to the summer we moved to New Orleans,
       to the yard where you are not even a shadow across the grass.

I will find August, the house beside the river,
              the blue flowers called Impatiens in the woodbox bed,
       my father's fence that keeps the men from the barges out.

I will find them again—those afternoons I hide
              in my house between the willow and the fence
       where I read the fairy tales stolen from my father's drawer.

I will reenter my favorite story, become again the girl
              in mourning shoes meeting the angel whose wings reach
       from his shoulders to the ground. He gives me a psalm, a broken

branch, and the red shoes. Then I disobey, escape—dance
              into the center of the forest. I am free and alone.
       When the angel finds me, he turns my bones to wood.

Outside the story I will live the longest summer
              of my life. Once, in my magic shoes, I will climb
       the metal fence, run to the river, make my father scared.

At the edge of the river I will press my heels into the sand,
              lean forward till the men on the barges wave.
       I am nine. I have never met you. I am doing the first

dangerous thing that will lead to you. Do you want to listen to my story?
              Is there a story that you want to hear? I'll tell you this—
       I am giving myself away. I am beginning the walk

toward you, in my slow measured steps. I am nine.
              I am fifteen. I am twenty. I am beginning to walk toward you
       without knowing you. Where are you in this long summer?

Do you ever go back to your own childhood? Do you have any story
       that you want to tell? This time, the first time, my father saves me.
    He calls me inside. The light falls and I turn to start for home.

I don't expect to find you on that path. Don't you see there is another world,
      there are other stories before yours and mine?

PASSION

*I am silent. I am silent, preparing
to join you again, earth.*
　　　　　　　　—Anna Akhmatova

I   SOLITUDE

I no longer want to be touched
in this life without you. The light falls

in my room, sharp as a knife. My dress
falls over my shoulders, over the bones

of my ribs. I want to grow smaller.
I want to prove that I can love you

without my body, as my aunts taught me
to love. The purest love: the grief

of abandonment. The sorrow that follows
departure. Not your hands on my throat,

in my hair, your voice speaking my name.
Where are you when I awake in the dark

with your letters, the photographs falling
over the sheets? You write, *Your body is imprinted*

on my hands. I hold you each night.
Then I lift my nightgown. I fill my body

with air. Listen. I speak to you alone.
Between us, the ocean lies, dull as lead.

II   THE ROBBER BRIDEGROOM

In this story, as my aunt tells it, the men cut
the woman's body into pieces. Their faces darken
with pleasure at the death of the newest bride.

My aunts and I sit in a circle in my room,
listening to the story we have heard before:
the crystal knife splits the throat open,

wine splashes on the table. This is the warning
about marriage, the warning that must be told
before I give myself away. Before I give myself

to this man they do not know. His body is incidental
to this lesson. It does not appear in their story,
handed down from the village in another country

where I have never been, first told in a house
I won't enter. In another century the storyteller
spreads her skirts on the bed and speaks

into darkness. The bride is trapped like an animal,
the men surround her in her room—

I turn from all of them, to begin our new life.

III   THE DOCUMENT

Kompong Cham, Cambodia

Your postcards are all lies. Tell the truth:
you are beginning to know fear. Show me

the photograph—in the field, the soldiers cut
the woman's hair. The knife is light against her shoulder.

Does she tell you this? Can you see her terror?
The knife teaches the danger of memory.

She tells you her husband's bones do not exist
in any grave. Only the document remains. Once,

he signed his name. *His voice.* I want
the photograph. You write, *She wants to live without*

him. No—she wants to live. At the edge
of the city, in the temple, the soldiers take apart the bodies

of the martyrs. Careful as surgeons, they touch
each statue, lifting the arm, the breast, the eye.

You study the survivors, walking over the field
where earth opened to receive them.

IV   RETRIEVAL

In my room I wait at my desk. I count
the things we will need in the next life:
passports, identity cards. *A declaration of intention.*
I wait for my aunts to appear

bearing the evidence, Rose's photograph, her signature,
husband's address unknown. What divides me
from her life? Why do I want that past? I want
to be the woman crossing the ocean to safety,

her fingers forming the letters of her new name
in the new language. *It is my intention to reside permanently.*
Why didn't the bride escape, follow a trail of ashes
to the end of the forest? Let me tell the truth.

V   DEVOTION

Each night in sleep you return to me.
In my dream, in the church, the window gives

back your face. In my dream, we give back our writing,
the pages of histories of women we will not see again.
We lay the pages on the steps of the altar and kneel

down together for the prayer. Raise the cup
of wine to your mouth. *This is my body.*
Ask for the resurrection of all the bodies.
This is my body which is given for you.

Let us be whole again.
Let us find our way back.
Let us both be far from our own deaths.

Lift my nightgown. Open my ribs with your hands.
I give myself up to you.

Love, let us be the witness. Listen. Nowhere is safe.

III   THE LAST CHILD OF THE TWENTIETH CENTURY

CENTURY OF PROGRESS

The Chicago World's Fair, 1933

Inside Montana a woman of pure silver stands,
hands held open in greeting like the Holy Mother.

At the entrance to California my grandmother finds
a knight dressed in a suit of armor made of prunes.

Costa Rica's pavilion offers chocolate coffee beans
and a lily five feet wide with the stiff ribs of an umbrella

that the man next to her says could fit a girl inside.
My grandmother walks alone to the Fairy Tale Village

where guides dress as wooden soldiers—no one
is thinking of war— past dinner plates the size

of pennies displayed in Tom Thumb's restaurant.
She is a girl of thirteen in a sailor dress marching on

to the Drama of Transportation, the hall of many
methods of escape: Egyptian chariots, horse and buggy,

a Henry Ford car. The highway of the future is a cloverleaf,
cars circling endlessly, and it is predicted that by 1980

every child will travel to school on a sky ride. We'll sit
on the beach of the moon in the dark, raising our glasses

of green ice, toasting the future in unison. In the New World
no one will ever want to die. My grandmother does not know

at the end of this century her three brothers will be gone
and she will be left with the unlucky women, with the family

sadness, the sickness. She won't give herself up to panic,
heart stuttering in her chest, won't practice the art of refusal,

a life without men. Like her I want to claim these virtues—
science and industry and progress, a hope for anything

approximating faith. We want the White City, the pavilion
filled with shining garages, bright marble porches, the Tower

of Jewels where flowers bloom from bird feathers
and a telescope transfixes moonlight. We beat our fists

on the door of the World of Tomorrow, demanding entry.
Now I live in the future no one wanted to forecast,

under the family tree, its branches snapped off.
Now I live in a story from childhood, from the past:

twelve princesses, sisters, slip from their beds to dance for a king
beneath their father's house. Under the earth each night they find

telegraphs, typewriters, inventions to deliver them from sickness,
to bring them to the Kingdom of Heaven. Let me deliver us.

Under the earth I lead my grandmother to the Palace
of Electricity, where the voltage lights up the sky like a movie screen.

Like the promise of Paradise.

FOR MY SISTER

Oh, you don't want to go back.
Once upon a time there were two sisters, the mad girl
and the other, the little one
under a golden counterpane, sleeping the Princess-sleep.
Little sugarplum, precious tea rose,
I'll drag you down the long hall of the past.
Up the back stairs where you hid your box of paints
(untouched, unspoiled like you, the cleanest Chinese White).
Through the kitchen, past the table set for three.
Out the front door, into the flood.
Look, I drive a cardboard box across the sidewalk
strewn with leaves, branches the storm snapped off.
Little girl, little girl, I'll let you come in . . .
Into the cardboard castle to share watercress
and tea from china thin as paper, thin as your skin.
Come, let me eat from your plate.
Let me drink from your cup.
Let me sleep beside you in your bed.
In our sinking ship we float away from the house,
you rowing with a green stick from the garden,
trying to save us. Don't save yourself.
I want to lose you, the undertow
of rainwater dragging you straight to the gutter.
I will be watching you.
I will be watching you disappear.
Give up your kingdom. Come with me
to the levee to see how high the river rises.
In my hand, behind my back, the jar,
its lid soaked with poison
(cotton stolen from your birthday box).
I look for crickets, families of fire ants
that crawl out after rain. Come closer, closer,
little one, make yourself small on the rim of the jar,
climb inside. The air is thick and sweet.
(The air smells like roses.)
Little girl, little girl, fly away home—
on the grass, the jar between my knees,
I am watching you.
Your house is on fire.
Little sister, little sister, let me come in.

Weak and fainting, you beat your wings
against the glass. What voice do you hear
calling you back, spinning magic through your sleep?
Nobody can help you now.
Give up your kingdom, your baby's breath.
I'll blow your house down.

THUMBELINA

I want to know where I can find a child
so I board the ship bound for the old

country. I cross over, back to the past
I never lived in, to the life that belonged

to my great-grandmother, the woman who started
the story my mother and I claim for ourselves.

I open the book written in script
on the shell of a barleycorn. Once, a flower

grew from this seed, a tulip, leaves tightly closed,
red and golden and locked shut, a secret.

Once, a woman pried the petals open
with her fingers to pick out a girl as tall

as her thumb. This is the child I need.
This is the child I will be able to save.

In a walnut half she sleeps the sleep
of comforted children, drifts on the surface

of a dinner plate. I must protect this girl
from the other world beneath this one.

Not from the men who want to claim her—
the toad, the fat mole—but from the fear

of the sun, from the desire for sickness.
In the underground world she'll learn

that nothing satisfies her body like the ache
of refusal, a slow burn in her stomach

as she waits at the table with her empty plate.
She wants to grow smaller. She won't sleep

till she circles the bridal chamber ninety-nine
times, engraving a path in the dirt to follow

each night. Above, a swallow beats its wings
on the earth, offering escape, offering to carry

her away to the Prince. She won't sleep until
she's invented her punishment: wrapping weeds

tight around her waist, tying her own hands
together with a piece of horsehair.

She fills her mouth with mud and kneels
on the floor. No—the child I'll find will live

on her own island, a water lily. She'll float
into the ocean. I'll take her in my hands

and, in the lit-up rooms of my own country,
here, at the end of this century,

I'll place her on my tongue. She drops
into my throat. For the first time she enters

my body. The swallow returns to its homeland,
to the window of my great-grandmother's house.

The book lies open on the table. My daughter
moves through my body. She swims

in my veins, touches the tips of my bones.
Out of this song comes our whole story.

THE SNOW QUEEN
AND THE GIBSON GIRL

for Daniel Gibson Knowlton

I

With my mandolin music, hatpins, my silver bicycle,
in my melon-sleeved wedding gown, I recline on the ice.
I dream I am driving an electric car into a wall
of water, sliding under the waves,
watching myself drown.

II

I have a sailor dress, a string ball
I unravel to lose count
of the days I have been dead.
I have been dead a long time now.

III

It's 1895. It's 1993. It is neither.
Here I am, in my American Beauty ballgown.
Oh, come back to me.
Put your arms around my neck.

IV

Hold my glass heart in your hands. Follow me.
There is no happiness here—
no sweetheart roses, no tea parties,
no games of kiss-in-the-ring.
The walls of my palace are made of snow.
The door is a wind.
The Northern Lights light up the halls,
more than a hundred halls.
You could get lost inside me.

V

In the center, a frozen lake
cracked into pieces, a Chinese puzzle of ice.
I spell out for you, *I am not the girl* . . .
The cracks spread inside me
taped with the white gauze of my gown.

VI

Come with me to my bedroom.
I'll show you the frozen mirror reflecting
only the worthless, the ugly,
those who are sad.
See how the beautiful shrink into nothing?
The good are too small to be seen.

VII

Here I am, framed in the glass beside the crows.
See the blackberries hung from the rotten tree.
There is no happiness here.

VIII

Step through the glass, answer me.
I am the white bee, the queen,
your bride in a bicycling costume.
I am not the girl

IX

Whose arms could hold you,
keep you safe.
I can't keep you.
Come to me. Come to me.

X

Who can put me back together again?

MAISON BLANCHE

My sister and I follow the long ruined avenue
to the end, where the traffic winds down
like a worn-out clock, ticking the minutes

till we can count on oblivion. Here, in this old
stone building, our great aunts sipped tea
as if it were gin, a parasol in every lady's glass,

wishing for ribbons and hatpins downstairs.
That was the year of gas-blue dresses, jet beads,
all the husbands leaving New Orleans for the war.

Now we are looking for our other sister, the middle child
who could complete the family, the only true bride.
Between the empty floors of shoes and organza dresses

we ride the wrought-iron elevator, the size of a coffin
built for two. Her grave was hand dug and shallow
so her soul would have room to float in the open sky.

Where is she, the one who could not escape
from our mother's body? We'll look behind the glass counter,
a jar of sugar sticks wrapped in lace,

inside the pot of artificial ferns by the door,
under the chenille of the showroom's brass bed.
Is she outside, one of the angels guarding the windows?

If this were my sister's dream, she and I would find
wedding dresses in the abandoned store. Twin brides,
we spin together on the stage on the third floor

while the milliner winds baby's breath into our hair.
In that dream I am completely safe.
I want to be the heroine in someone else's story

but my own dream has nothing to do with refuge
or safety or a man gripping my shoulders.
In this other world I don't wish for a man who can save us.

Instead I want us alone, holding her small wire bones
till the rib cage lifts from her body,
the rib cage opens like an exhibit to reveal a family

of children in white dresses, all the unborn girls who know
shame and disgrace, now delivered.

THE LAST NIGHT OF THE TWENTIETH CENTURY

for my mother

I LOS ALAMOS, 1950

The sisters stare into the sun. This is the cure
for the girl who will become my mother, the girl
born with eyes that fail and a sister who wants that failure

for herself. At the edge of the blue kidney-shaped pool
my mother offers her face to the sky like a lover,
eyes held open while her father's cigarette burns to ash

between his fingers. In the story he tells his daughters
each night a silver plane touches down in a field
to save sad children and the bomb is nothing

more than a low hum in the throat, a constant music
like the panic one of his daughters will choose
as her faith. My mother's eyes burn. He tells her

under the earth below her is a shelter, a safehouse,
and a line of girls in gas masks, no fear visible
in their faces. This summer, her father teaches her

the word for *future* in four languages, words
from the old country. He holds her face in his hands.

This is the summer he teaches her how to die.

II NEW ORLEANS, 1966

She does not understand the punishment.
This is the day I will enter my mother's life,

the first child to share her body.
In the hospital the doctors prepare her

for the event: the gas that smells like lemons,
the pressure of the razor between her legs.

If I were beside her, I would soak
bandages for her eyes to turn her gaze to a safe

darkness. In the operating theater's silver
light my mother begins an inventory

of her body before sleep, before she will no longer
be alone with it: breasts, hips, wrists to circle

with two fingers. She doesn't know this, but for her,
I am willing to disappear. I want to say,

go on without me. Don't look. I am willing
to give up my body for you. I say, forget me,

and like an angel she rises from the white bed.

III   ODESSA, 1925

In the village on the border between two countries
your father belongs nowhere.
Your father is walking
in the middle of the road, identity papers folded
in his pocket. He is nine and does not yet know
the new language of the twentieth century:
the words for *transport, homeland, Zyklon-B.*
Fifteen years later, the locked railway cars
will sway along these tracks,
leading the citizens of his village to their "new life."
Fifteen years later, in another country,
he will be a man beginning to leave his daughters
to survive without him in the other world.

IV   THE FUTURE

Under the earth, Mother, I am waiting.
I watch for you in the dark.
Your father has come back to offer directions.
He sets a stone from Russia in my mouth.

Under the earth, I cannot locate the past.
What I find is the future: a stone on the tongue.
A nail dropped in the soup for iron. Holy water.

On television the prophets argue about a doom
we have expected. Whose punishment will be first?
The damned, the saved, the ones who live in fear?

In this world there will be no more children.
I write your name in ash on the sand.
The world has no more miracles.

This is the night when I inhabit your body.

ALICE IN PARADISE

I

Tonight, Sister, I'll call you back to me, to the bed
where I lie still after passion, returned to my own body,

restored to myself and alone. Enter me
like a lover, hands fluttering between my ribs,

curl up inside me, pale as a root, white fish
that would fit in a shoe box, an angel under my skin.

Together we'll go down to the place where no man
can take me, through the rooms of our parents' house,

past silver-framed photographs that do not include you,
past the table where you never sat.

Mother is only a word as we climb down to darkness.

II

In the story the girl has time to prepare
for the descent into the country she knows no name for.

What she knows: the passage out of this world
does not lead to light but spins to the center

of the earth, where teacups rattle on hooks in the dirt
and the shelves are crowded with books with blank pages.

Tell me a story, she'd said with no fear,
and the man who loved her invented her life.

You see, the path to God is no worse than a fall down the stairs.

III

In the fenced-off part of the Garden of Memories
where we buried you, none of the children lived more

than three days. None of the children have names:
Baby Smith, Baby Miller, Baby Taylor, Baby.

If you had ever breathed, you would have been given my name,
and I could imagine you, namesake, a rubber doll swinging

through Paradise, running free in the land of the old.
Now I look for your small stone, the marker

the size of a book pointing the way to oblivion.
You will be the first child to live in my body.

Fill my lungs like water, suck in my breath.

IV

Always ahead, Alice picks the yellow hearts of daisies,
twisting the stems into a chain to form a path.

I can't find the rabbit hole, the road dropping down
to the country of childhood, and inside me

you move restlessly like a fever.
The world is failing you again. I am failing to save you

and all night I will look for that tree
where the girl-child sat solemnly, the book in her lap,

dreaming of griffins and queens. If I give up
on this magic, will I lose you again?

I cannot let myself rest. Below us, in the other kingdom,
Alice drinks from the bottle with the paper label, patiently

waits at the door to grow small. I am waiting.
Sister, tell me the secrets you learned without me,

teach me the lessons of the unborn, the story of fear,
and I will listen as your voice fills my throat, one note,

the sound of our name, breathless, unaccompanied.

SLEEPING BEAUTY IN THE AQUARIUM

In the saltwater tank
I have been awake for a hundred years.
Lying in my gold-plated coffin,
a pirate's treasure chest,
I keep my eyes open to scare
the children, to find my mother
when she comes back to see her secret
dredged up from the deep
cold water below the horizon.

The visitors nod and smile,
move on to the outdoor shark tank,
to the octopus with thirteen legs
on the reef labeled Freaks of Nature.
My label: Lost Maiden Preserved in Salt.

And the rest of this story?
Not my mother's grief, not
her desire for a child
that filled the court.
No one saw my mother sitting sullen
at the christening party
drinking wine from a ruby glass.

No one sees her when she finds me
at the spinning wheel
and shuts my eyes with straight pins.
In the middle of the night she drags
me out to sea, weighting my body
with stones from the castle garden.

I'm restless on my golden bed.
When she appears
my mother will direct the crowd
to the exhibit of sunken ships.
She'll point out the graceful
damselfish, the seahorses . . .

I wait for her return.
I'll rise up to greet her
at the underwater window.

Mother, there is room for no one else
in this story but you and me,
the story that will have no errors,
the story the castle scribe is writing for me
in tiny, perfect script
on the head of a pin.

HELEN KELLER, NEW ORLEANS

In my bed I imagine Helen singing like an angel.
She has not spoken her song out loud to anyone before.

In her story each letter is repeated, tapped out on the flat of the hand.
My angel, princess, magic girl, we exist in darkness.

Beside the well Helen waits in her silence,
Anne pumping water into her hand.

We will begin with the simplest words: *air, fire, water*.
I say *mother* and she appears. She climbs into my bed.

Like a thief I crawl out the bedroom window to follow
my mother to the front lawn, to the car that will take us

away from my father. *We are going to New Orleans.*
My mother is good at a lie. In the motel guest book I sign *Helen*.

These are my mother's last instructions: stay far away
from the window, don't let men see you, sleeping is not safe.

I see my father stumbling through the empty rooms of our house
in the city, turning on all the lights to find us.

I see my mother leaving me in the motel while she drives back
to save him. With the suitcases stacked against the door I could stay

locked up forever, free and alone. Helen's lesson of childhood—
sing to yourself and the past sings back.

Helen sings to me that her mother is dead and together
we enter her magic world, the kingdom of little girls,

the Kingdom of Heaven, the heaven with no mothers.
Kingdom of childhood, I want to blow you down.

I splinter the walls of the castle. I flood the bedrooms
till water rises to the ceiling. I drown the King in his golden bed.

He is suffocated under the magic counterpane.
I lock the Queen in the tower.

In my bed my mother and I turn together in the separate countries
of our bodies. *We are going to New Orleans.*

We will never talk about her leaving me. We will never talk
about how each time, for years, she rescued my father.

The princess packs her suitcase with dresses.
The princess jumps into the well and is gone.

I walk out of childhood as out of a theater,
blinking into light. No one is singing.

Tell me, Mother, what is this word you taught me,
the word you won't spell out in my hand, the word for grief?

THE FAMILY HISTORY

In the sister's garden it is still winter
when the boy who will be my father follows her
between the spines of trees, down the dark path.

In his mother's house on the shore of Lake Michigan
where one room opens onto another with no place
to find refuge, his sister comes after him, chases

him from one closet to the next, drags him out
from under the bed. Their bodies knock together.
This is not an embrace. He is a trespasser

into her life. "My garden is my own garden."
On his arm the scab from last night opens like a bloom.
No one alive will tell me this story, you see, but I'm here,

hidden on the roof of the castle, behind the leaves
shaped like stars. I have come to help my father find
the way out of childhood, the long road that will lead

to oblivion. I never saw a photograph of this scene
but I know enough to tell the boy, if you find a cottage
in a clearing in the woods, it's not safe, don't stop.

My garden is my own garden. I know the day
she pushes his face under the ice of the lake
till his body stops shuddering, his hands float

to the surface. And I know his dreams about animals:
a frog waiting on a bed of damask roses, a centaur,
crocuses wound in its horns, who can rescue him

with the promise of Paradise where he'll be alone.
His sister wears flowers wound in her braids
and holds him down on her bed till he cries mercy.

Father, come with me, I see the prints of two nails
on your palms, the prints of two nails on your feet.
The golden ball lies in the mud at the bottom

of the well. The single pea is buried under stacks
of counterpanes. You won't find it, but in the backyard
rows of red poppies will send you off to sleep.

My garden is my own garden. The trees aren't women
who lean toward you in the wind. There is no salvation.
Father, listen. You won't know the way back.

RESURRECTION

for Rose Marlovits Raden (1897–1978)

I

In my story the sisters forecast bad weather.
Twins born during the first harvest signal luck.

My great-grandmother and her sister are the magicians
of a town that never appears on a map of Hungary.

After her predictions of the peasant women's fertility,
after she warns of a drought that will burn the fields to dust,

after she's confessed the sins and graces of every citizen,
the priest holds the cup to my great-grandmother's lips

and the history of the women in this family unfolds—
scissors, table knives, razor blades skimming our wrists,

the wire to bite in the hospital driving lightning up the spine,
the solitude we refuse to call loneliness, the sickness

that rises again and again in our throats, the vinegar
to keep ourselves thin. My great-grandmother knows our story,

the story of the sisters who will follow her into the next world.

II

In Budapest, the traveling photographer mounts pictures
of dead children in albums, saving a lock of hair for each book.
Wearing dark dresses, matching handkerchiefs pressed
flat to the collarbone, the twins sit together, they wait.

When he holds the iron to their hair, steam rises over
their faces. The sisters hold still. Inside the frame
of the daguerreotype, pain isn't visible. No one in this city
knows the sisters. No one knows that one of us

will drink cologne in order to die. In the unnamed village
a coin with a double image still signifies luck.

III

In the New World, she beats the egg stiff for a strudel
and remembers synchronized steps across the potato fields,
arm in arm with her sister, their magic linked up.

In Europe angels guarded the beds of the dying.
The angels left my great-grandmother to cross
the ocean alone to her new life. The angels don't know

that I'll resurrect all the sisters. As the train
from Ellis Island drags along the horizon, the priest
lifts the bread and the wine to the mouths of the women

who ask for forgiveness, who plead for a safe, early death.

IV

Rose, when you come back to this world I'll be waiting,
suitcase at my side, with my camera, to follow you

to the next unnamed village, to find the last child
of the twentieth century, drowned in the well.

We rub matchsticks over her eyebrows. We paint
circles of rouge on her cheeks. We scorch each

of her curls with the iron. We fill her mouth with vinegar.
Together we prepare the girl for the Kingdom of Heaven.

In the country lit up by a powder flash of the camera,
the ashes that mark the sisters are blessed with the curse

you cast before you disappeared forever—your punishment,
Life Everlasting.

THE AFTERLIFE

St. Malo, France

On this trip I expected you'd come back.
I prayed for your return, as the long black body

of the train cut through winter fields. I wanted you
to find me in the walled city where, once,

soldiers' voices echoed at the edge of the water,
one word, then another, exploding. Now

below us cannons rust on the ocean floor.
I looked for you when I walked with him

through streets where sailors stand at the zinc bar
in every lighted doorway to follow women

with their eyes. I whispered your name,
a warning. Yesterday, this man and I began

our life together. We began to speak
in our own language. I offered him my grief,

the panic that rises in my throat, my desire
to be another woman, a heroine, in a new story

told with the words I pull through my hands like rope.

*

Rose, let me follow you through the city
to the beach, sand blank as paper, where boats begin
the crossing to the other country.

Lead me to the ship with no staterooms
or tour guides, the ship crowded with women
who want to escape the war.
In our family, women learn to master escape.

Show me the village where land is passed on
from father to son, where you wait at the well

with your sisters, passing buckets
from hand to hand through rows of dry wheat.

Here is your husband's ax breaking open the field.
Here are his hands that hold you down.
Here is the life that makes you choose exile.

I want to walk out with you into your life.
I want to walk into the water that divides past
from future. You leave Hungary with your wedding ring
sewn in the hem of your dress and the hope
of a man who won't hurt you.

*

In the Hotel Neptune, my hands move over his body.
I kiss the knots in his spine, one by one.
When I open his rib cage with my tongue, I am speaking

your language. If I could spell fear with your alphabet
I would be safe. The white sheet on this bed is worn
from the pressure of hundreds of bodies.

In the next world, the rooms are full of nothing
but bodies. The afterlife is full of women:
your mother, your sisters, your daughters who escaped.

Who can tell which of us will give in? I have chosen
this man. His name is a word that drifts on my tongue.
Rose, come to me. Fill the bath with salt water.

Push your bone pins into my hair. Slip the white dress
over my head, the dress heavy with shells.
Prepare my body for love. Open the earth to receive us.